Community Gardens in Community
Libraries
Funded by a
Library Services & Technology Act (LSTA) grant

CITY OF
RIVERSIDE

Riverside Public Library

Earth Matters

A+ books

WHAT'S SPROUTING IN MY TRASH?

A Book about Composting

by Esther Porter

Content Consultant:
Tom Fitz, PhD
Associate Professor of Geoscience
Northland College
Ashland, Wisconsin

CAPSTONE PRESS
a capstone imprint

Do you like to recycle? Earth does too! In fact, nature has taught us a great deal about recycling. Earth knows how to renew itself naturally. **If we watch closely, we can learn too.**

4

Compost is nature's way of recycling. In autumn, a tree's leaves fall to the ground. The leaves' energy goes back into the dirt. Now Earth can use the energy again. **It might even go back into the tree it came from.**

Nature never loses energy, thanks to a few little helpers in the ground called microorganisms. Micro-*what*? Microorganisms!

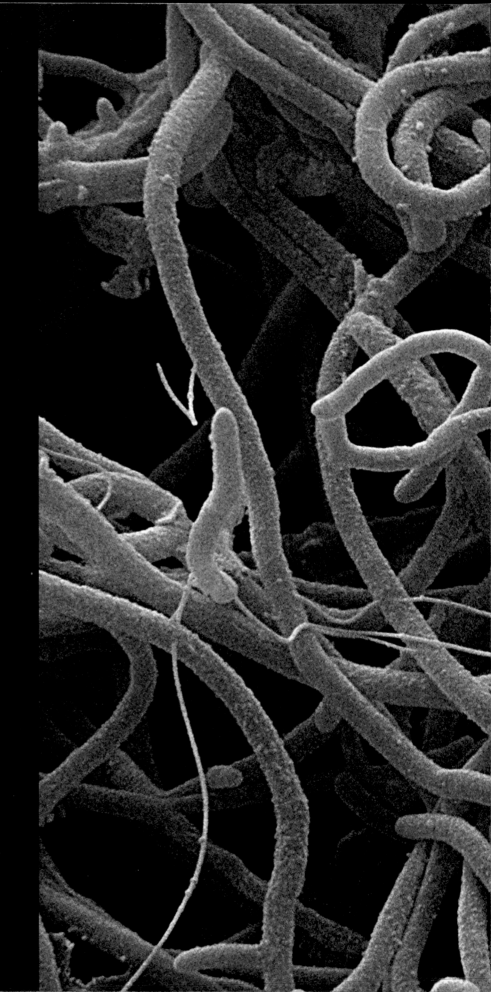

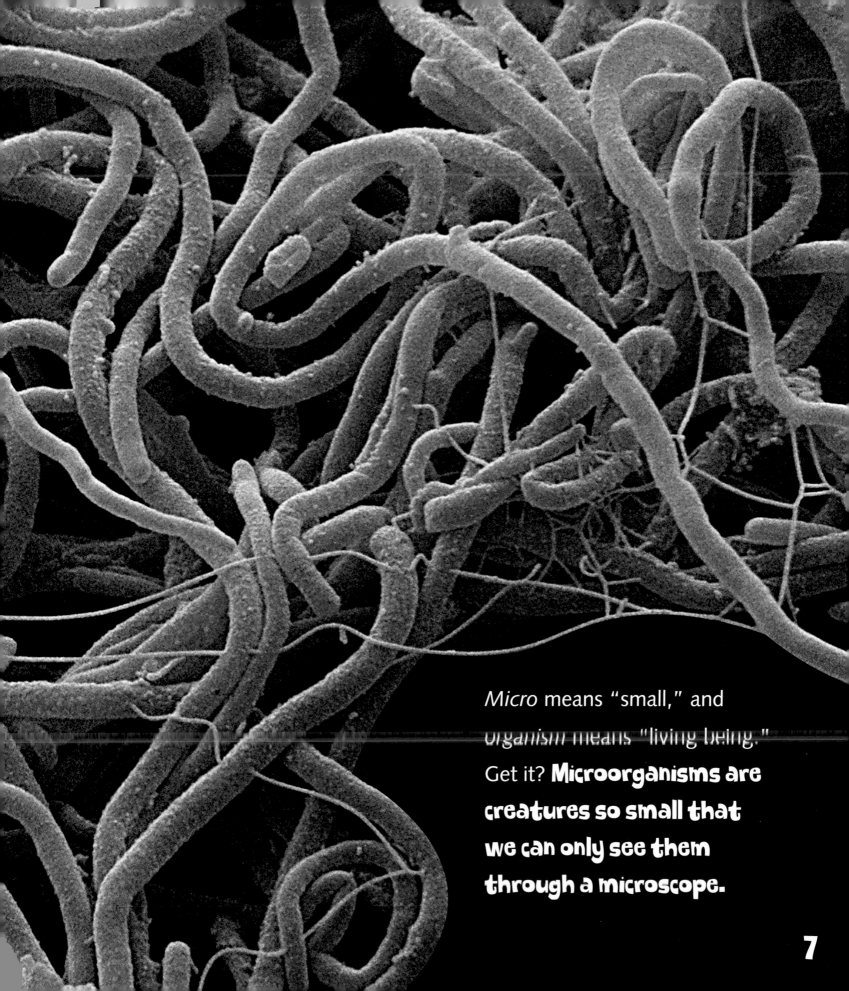

Micro means "small," and *organism* means "living being." Get it? **Microorganisms are creatures so small that we can only see them through a microscope.**

With the help of larger critters like worms and bugs, microorganisms eat almost everything that falls to the ground. **In fact, when plants and animals die, microorganisms have a feeding frenzy.**

As they eat, microorganisms take in energy. They keep a little for themselves, and the rest of the energy goes back into the ground. **The microorganisms' work turns trash into a super rich mix called humus.**

The breakdown of energy happens slowly in nature, but it happens quickly in compost. Compost can be kept in a bin or in a pile on the ground. It can be small or big. **There are many ways to make compost, but a few things are needed for it to work well.**

Compost needs the right ingredients. Grass clippings, leaves, and shredded newspaper are good. **Kitchen scraps like banana peels and eggshells are perfect for compost.**

15

Don't add meat to compost. Meat attracts dogs, cats, raccoons, and other animals that would dig through it. **We don't want those critters hurting themselves or the compost pile.**

Just like people, compost needs air. Oxygen keeps away stinky bacteria, and it feeds the good bacteria. Keep compost nice and fluffy and full of air. How? **Just mix it!**

Compost also
needs the right
amount of water.
If there's too much water,
the air can't reach the little
helpers in the pile. If there's too little,
the microorganisms can dry out and die.
**The best compost has a perfect
mix of water and air.**

Compost stays healthy
when it is kept warm. As good
bacteria zip around feasting on trash,
they create their own heat. When
it is warm, the ingredients quickly
break apart. **This speeds up the
compost process.**

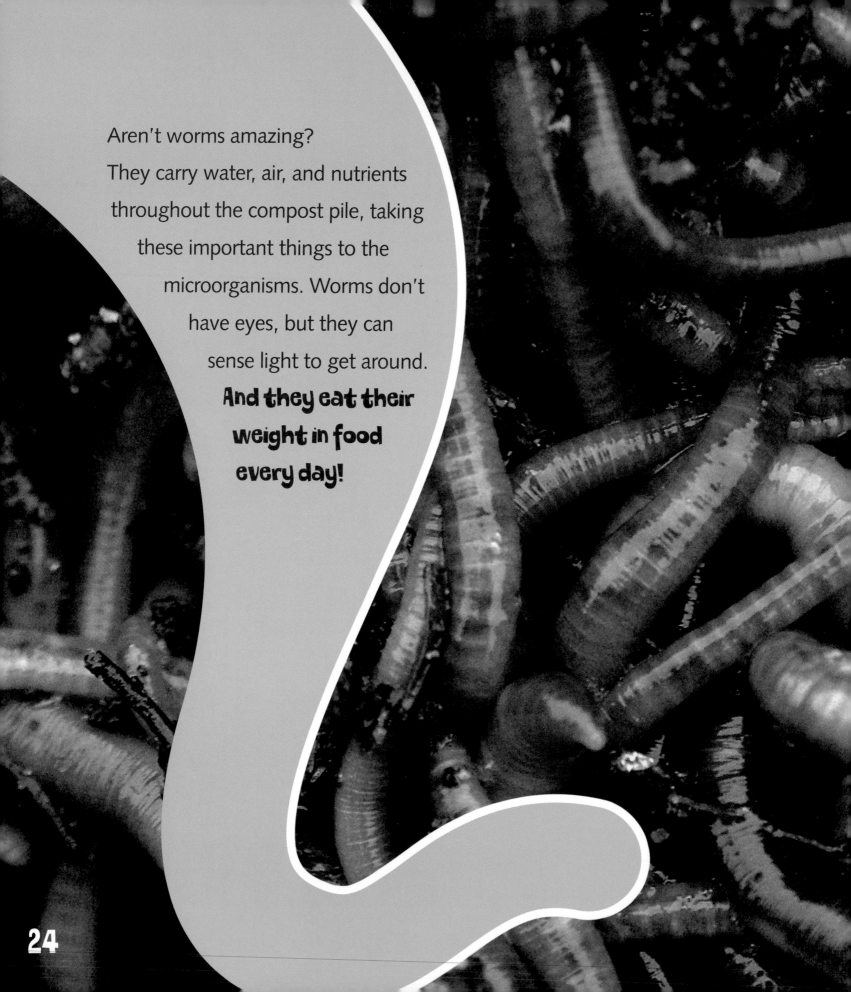

Aren't worms amazing? They carry water, air, and nutrients throughout the compost pile, taking these important things to the microorganisms. Worms don't have eyes, but they can sense light to get around. **And they eat their weight in food every day!**

When we compost,
we have less trash to dump in
our landfills. Compost also acts as a
filter for Earth and prevents pollution
from spreading. **When we allow nature
to teach us, our planet is a happier
and more beautiful place to live.**

27

Composting in a Jar

Want to see how compost works? Make compost in a jar! Like a compost pile or bin, compost in a jar turns scraps and clippings into perfect compost. Here's how to make your own:

You will need:

large clear plastic or glass jar
food scraps (fruit peels, bread)
leaves
grass clippings
garden soil (not potting soil)

Instructions:

Place 2 inches (5 centimeters) of soil in the bottom of a plastic or glass jar. Moisten for best results. Place food scraps, leaves, and grass clippings on top of the soil in several, repeating layers. Leave the jar open and place on a windowsill or other location where it will not be disturbed.

Check the jar daily. What changes do you see?
Add a little water every week. Mix it by stirring.
When your compost is broken down into dark,
rich soil, add it to a garden or planter.

Glossary

bacteria—tiny, single-celled creatures that exist everywhere in nature

compost—mixture of decaying leaves, vegetables, and other items that make the soil better for gardening

energy—the ability to do work, such as giving heat or light

humus—rich soil full of energy and nutrients

landfill—a place where garbage is buried

microorganism—a living thing too small to be seen without a microscope

nutrient—a substance needed by a living thing to stay healthy

oxygen—a colorless gas that people breathe; compost needs oxygen to break down

pollution—materials that hurt Earth's water, air, and land

recycle—to make used items into new products; nature recycles dead leaves into new energy

Read More

Glaser, Linda. *Garbage Helps Our Garden Grow: A Compost Story.* Minneapolis: Millbrook Press, 2010.

Koontz, Robin Michal. *Composting: Nature's Recyclers.* Amazing Science. Minneapolis: Picture Window Books, 2007.

Siddals, Mary McKenna. *Compost Stew: An A to Z Recipe for the Earth.* Berkeley, Calif.: Tricycle Press, 2010.

Internet Sites

FactHound offers a safe, fun way to find Internet sites related to this book. All of the sites on FactHound have been researched by our staff.

Here's all you do:

Visit *www.facthound.com*

Type in this code: 9781620650479

 Check out projects, games and lots more at **www.capstonekids.com**

Index

A+ Books are published by Capstone Press,
1710 Roe Crest Drive, North Mankato, Minnesota 56003
www.capstonepub.com

Library of Congress Cataloging-in-Publication Data
The Cataloging-in-Publication information is on file with the Library of Congress.
ISBN: 978-1-62065-047-9 (library binding)
ISBN: 978-1-62065-745-4 (paperback)
ISBN: 978-1-4765-1095-8 (eBook PDF)

Editorial Credits
Jeni Wittrock, editor; Bobbie Nuytten, designer; Svetlana Zhurkin, media researcher;
Jennifer Walker, production specialist

Photo Credits
Dreamstime: Geoffrey Carrascalao Heard, 24–25; Getty Images: David Scharf, 6–7; Shutterstock: Alex
Staroseltsev, 1 (top), andersphoto, cover (right), 1 (right), c. (cardboard texture), cover (top), Christian De Araujo,
28 (grass), Christine Norton, 22–23, danzo80, 5 (leaves graphic), eddtoro, 16–17, gcpics, 14–15, HomeStudio, 28
(jar), Jeff Gynane, 12–13, Julija Sapic, 20–21, M. Cornelius, 18–19, Mares Lucian, 10–11, marslander, 28 (banana
peel), Miao Liao, 4–5, Monkey Business Images, 29, Morgan Lane Photography, 2–3, Pakhnyushcha, 8–9,
pashabo (recycled paper texture), cover and throughout, Richard Griffin, 28 (scoop with soil), sanddebeautheil,
cover (left), Sandra van der Steen, 28 (leaves), Sarunyu_foto, 26–27, Valery Kraynov, 28 (back), 30–31, 32

Note to Parents, Teachers, and Librarians
This Earth Matters book uses full color photographs and a nonfiction format to introduce the concept of
earth science and is designed to be read aloud to a pre-reader or to be read independently by an early reader.
Photographs help listeners and early readers understand the text and concepts discussed. The book encourages
further learning by including the following sections: Glossary, Read More, Internet Sites, and Index. Early
readers may need assistance using these features.

Printed in the United States of America in North Mankato, Minnesota.
092012   006933CGS13